Whiskered Words of Frisky Felines

Shelby Kent-Stewart
R.J. Pickrell, Illustrator

Wordsmiths, Ink LLC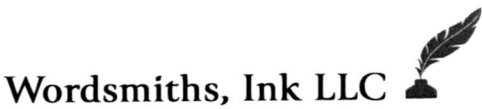

Published by Wordsmiths, Ink, Gilbert, AZ

This is a work of fiction. Names, characters, places, and incidents are the product of the author's imagination and have been used to create this work of art. Any similarity to actual persons, living or dead, events, etc. is completely coincidental.

All rights reserved. Copyright © 2025 Shelby Kent-Stewart

Cover image copyright © Shelby Kent-Stewart

No part of this book may be reproduced or transmitted in any form or by any means, electronic or mechanical, including photocopying, recording, or by any information storage and retrieval system, permitted by law. For information contact: Wordsmiths, Ink, Gilbert, AZ

ISBN

Hardcover
9798999502995

This book is dedicated to the millions of cat lovers who understand the alternate universe in which our fabulous felines exist to keep us entertained.

Special thanks to Shirlee Laughlin, whose support and encouragement made this book a joy to write.

With love and thanks to R.J. Pickrell for the brilliant illustrations that brought our frisky felines to life.

Table of Contents

Cats: 1-75

Cat Vocabulary: 76

DIY Cat Toys: 77

Cat Shelters: 78-80

Hell no, I didn't volunteer for this and my name's not Dave!

I'm beautiful.   I'm smart.   I'm trouble.

My human thinks I'm special. Who am I to disagree?

Inspector Whiskers here. If some damn fool posts my photo on Facebook and blows my cover, there'll be hell to pay.

I saved your Jimmy Chew from the dog!
A little gratitude would be nice.

She rescued a dog?!!! Relax, Ralph. We wait until she leaves the house and then he's toast.

I'm bored. You have 10 seconds to snap the photo or I'm outta here.

Nope, I'm hiding here until she stops screaming at the nightly news or passes out from too many martinis.

Bring it on, winged devil. Make my day.

Chill, dude. A quick snip, a cone around your neck for a few days and you'll be good as new.

You've dressed me as an elf, a leprechaun and witch that made me twitch. I get that you're conflicted but henceforth you're restricted, so unless you're prepared to grease my paw with money, remember I'm a feline not a bunny.

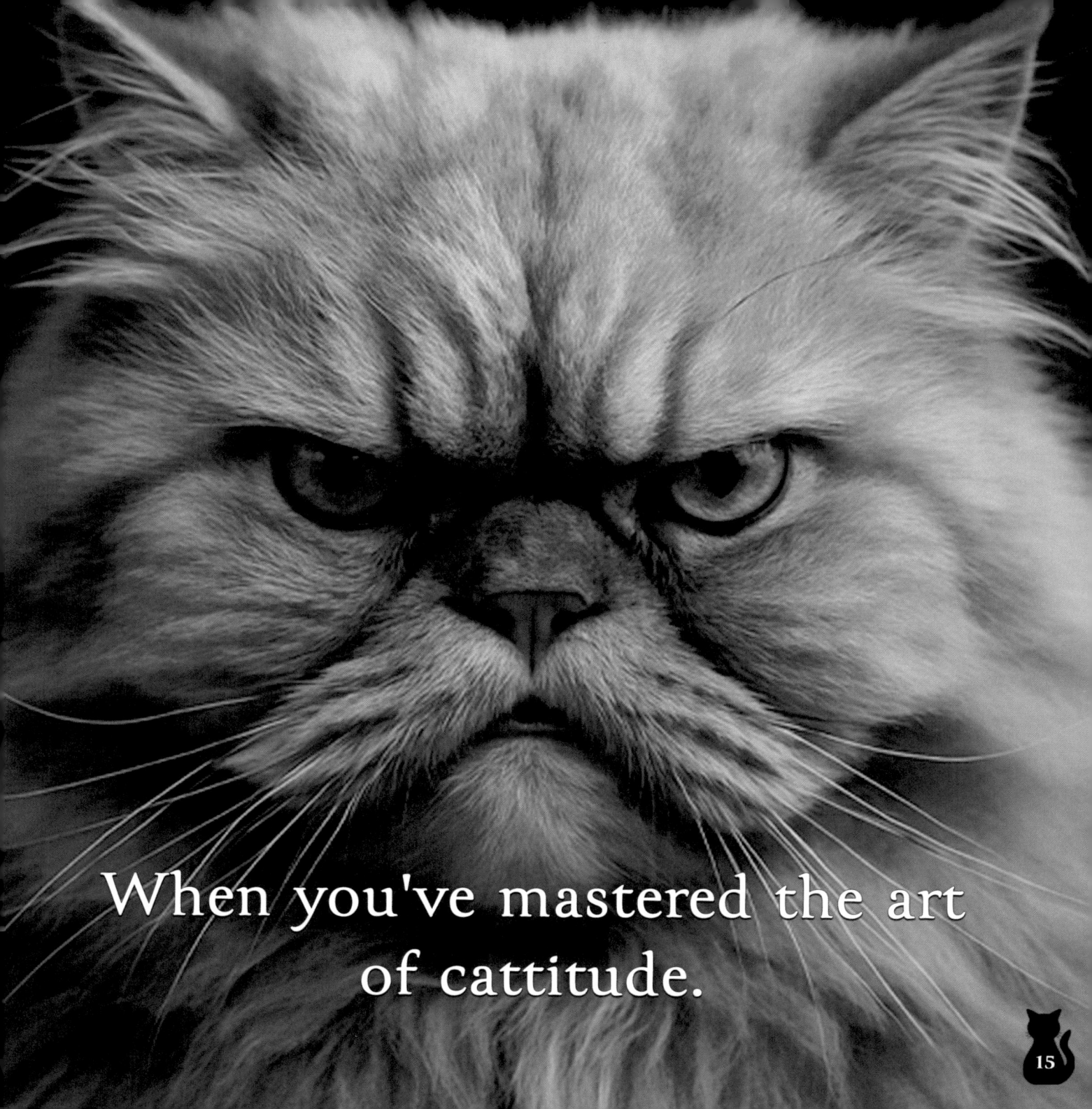

Really? We're still doing the Hello Kitty thing?

The Vampire Lescat?! Nope, no way. Next?

Captain Cat Sparrow?! Oh, hell no. Next?

You'll pay for this, human.
Count on it.

I can't do it. He's so cute and fuzzy with whiskers just like me.

A little help would be nice. Did I forget to mention I got the fly?

Copy that. Operation scare the crap out of the human is a go.

No, I don't want to talk about it, but that's the last time I'm partying with the cougars.

I found him at the dog park.
Can I keep him?

"Let's hang out," he said.
"It'll be fun," he said.

Had you thought this through and named me Mozart instead of Muffin, perhaps I'd be a bit more inspired.

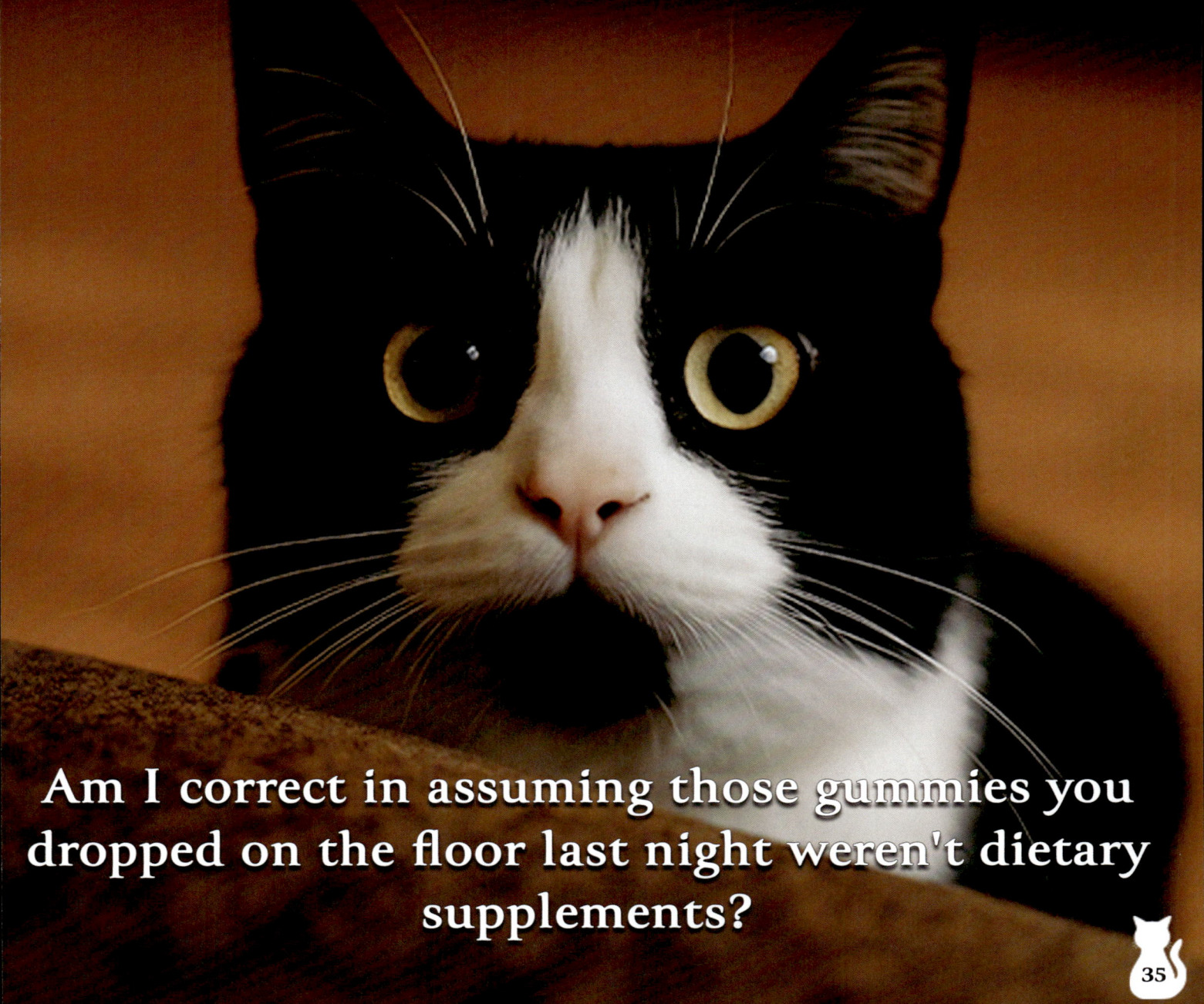

We've talked about this, human. You sprinkle baking soda in my litter box again and the parakeet is history.

Remember that unfortunate incident with your Louboutins? You may want to keep that in mind if you're thinking of sharing this humiliating photo on social media.

You say 'cat ladies' like it's a bad thing. What's up with that?

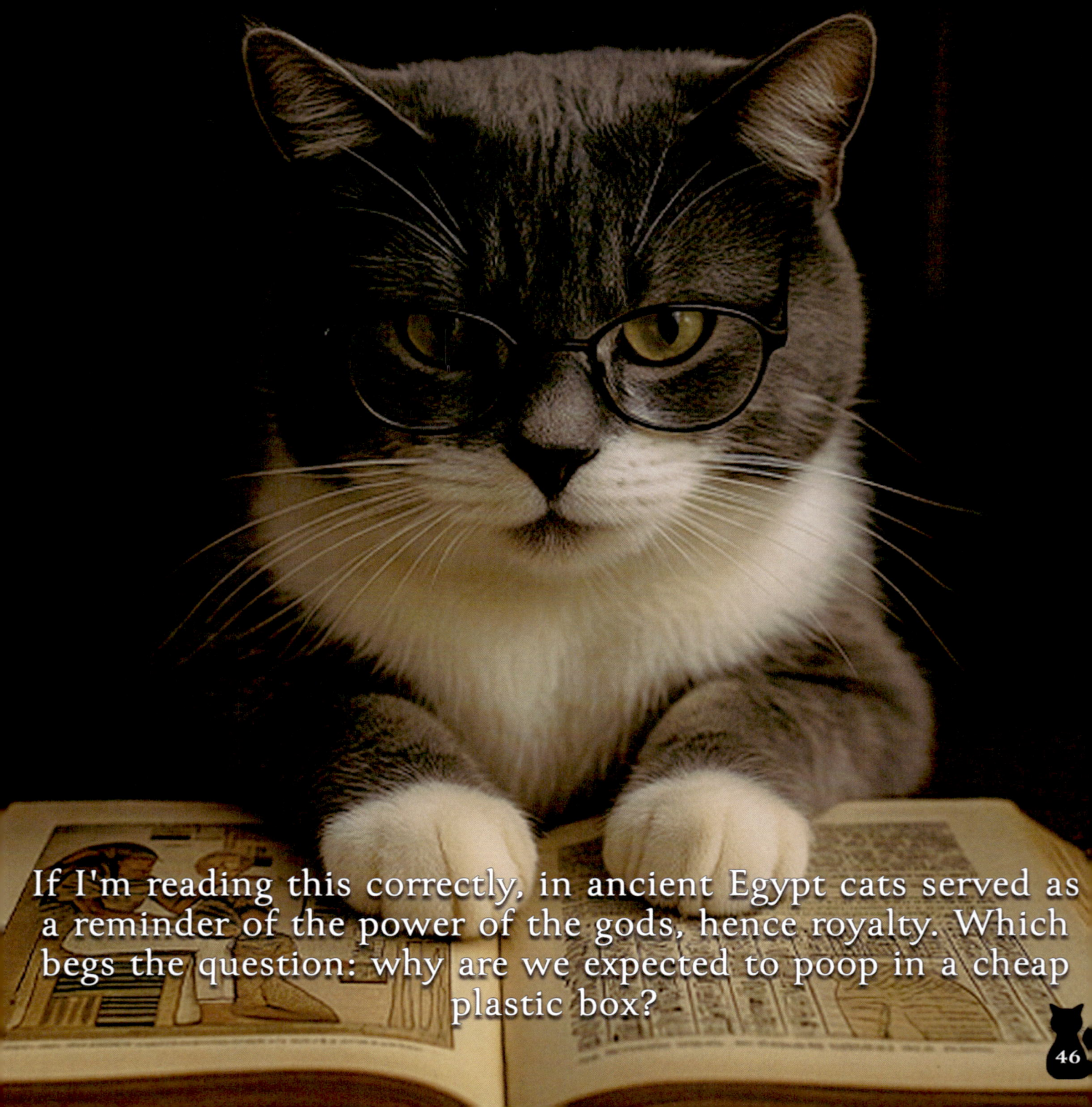

Oh, hell no. While I indulge your obsession with costumes, I draw the line at executing a pirouette.

I hate to complain, but whoever put humans in charge down here may want to rethink that decision.

I'll be your best friend forever if you take me with you. Planet Earth is a hot mess.

Humans are weird. You'd think a guy who calls himself Santa Claws would have the good sense to put on fake ones...and don't even get me started on the beard.

Who's the wiseguy who nominated me as Santa for Feline Festivus?

Not it! If you're determined to bathe something, you'll find the dog in the alley humping the neighbor's poodle.

Is it just me or does the fact that humans are running things scare the poop out of you?

Pull yourself together, Blanche. The film version of CATS was released six years ago, and most of us have survived the humiliation.

Nice campsite but would it have killed them to offer room service?

Cat Vocabulary Glossary

Attack Wiggle – The dramatic pre-pounce butt shimmy. Nature's most adorable warning sign.

Blep – The adorable, unexplained appearance of a tiny tongue tip. Causes instant human meltdown.

Boop – A gentle poke to the nose, usually met with judgment and disdain.

Cattitude – An unapologetic, sass-heavy state of being. Often accompanied by side-eyes.

Chirp – The strange birdlike sound cats make when hunting... through a closed window.

Clawditor – A cat who walks across your keyboard with edits of their own.

Crinkle Freakout – The chaotic frenzy triggered by a paper bag or crinkly wrapper.

Flop – Sudden, exaggerated collapse in front of you. A test of devotion and snack availability.

Furnado – The swirling cloud of hair unleashed during every grooming session.

Ghost Nap – That eerie moment when your cat stares at nothing, then falls asleep mid-hover.

Loafing – When a cat tucks in all limbs and looks like a perfectly baked bread loaf.

Mlem – A single, deliberate lick of the air. Usually when absolutely nothing justifies it.

Murder Mittens – Fluffy paws concealing razor-sharp vengeance. Often deployed during "play."

Pawditude – The unshakable belief that all furniture, food, and sunlight belongs to them.

Purrito – A cat tightly wrapped in a blanket. May look cute. Still armed.

Scritch-spot – A mysteriously specific place where pets are suddenly acceptable.

Slow Blink – The feline equivalent of "I love you." Or "You may continue existing."

Sploot – When a cat lays flat with back legs splayed behind. Equal parts regal and ridiculous.

Void Mode – When your black cat disappears into the shadows and becomes a trip hazard.

Zoomies – A spontaneous burst of 300 mph energy, typically executed at 3:00 am on hardwood floors for maximum drama.

DIY Cat Toys & Treat Recipes

T-Shirt Yarn Wand Toy
What You Need:
- An old cotton t-shirt
- A stick or dowel
- Scissors
- Hot glue or string

Instructions:
1. Cut the t-shirt into long strips (about 1 inch wide).
2. Tie several strips together at one end.
3. Secure that end to your stick with glue or wrap it tightly with more fabric/string.
4. Wiggle it like it owes your cat money.

Pro Tip: The more aggressive your cat's tail flick, the better your craftsmanship.

TUNA & CATNIP BITES
Ingredients:
- 1 can tuna in water (drained)
- 1 tbsp dried catnip
- 1 egg
- 2 tbsp oat flour (or blend oats until fine)

Instructions:
1. Preheat oven to 350°F (175°C).
2. Mix all ingredients into a dough.
3. Roll into tiny balls and flatten slightly.
4. Bake on a parchment-lined tray for 10–12 mins.
5. Cool completely. Store in fridge for up to 5 days.

Chef's Note: If your cat suddenly calls you "Chef," act natural.

FROZEN FISHY CUBES
Ingredients:
- Tuna water or low-sodium chicken broth
- A few bits of cooked shredded chicken or fish

Instructions:
1. Pour liquid into an ice cube tray.
2. Drop in a little bit of protein.
3. Freeze.
4. Pop one out for a cooling summer treat!

Bonus: It's like a spa day. But fishier.

TOILET PAPER ROLL PUZZLE
What You Need:
- Empty toilet paper roll
- Small cat treats or dry food
- Tape or glue
- Scissors

Instructions:
1. Fold both ends of the roll inward to close one side.
2. Add a few treats inside.
3. Close the other side but leave a small gap or poke holes.
4. Watch your cat suddenly become an escape-room champion.

Level Up: Add multiple rolls together to form a mega puzzle tube.

Cat Shelters

Alabama
Montgomery Humane Society
800 Professional Dr, Montgomery, AL 36116
(334) 270-2699
montgomeryhumane.com

Alaska
Alaska Humane Society
5450 Nunaka Valley Rd, Anchorage, AK 99508
(907) 344-2020
adopt-a-cat.org

Arizona
Arizona Animal Welfare League (AAWL)
25 N 40th St, Phoenix, AZ 85034
602-273-6852
aawl.org

Arkansas
Needy Paws Animal Shelter
1040 E Main St, Clarksville, AR 72830
(479) 754-7387
needypawsanimalshelter.org

California
D.E.L.T.A. Rescue
1500 La Tuna Canyon Rd, Acton, CA 93510
deltarescue.org

Colorado
Rocky Mountain Feline Rescue
2390 S. Delaware St., Denver, CO 80223
(303) 691-6008
rmfr-colorado.org

Connecticut
Animal Friends of CT
401 Washington St., New Britain, CT 06051
(860) 377-9991
animalfriendsofct.org

Delaware
Humane Animal Partners
701 A Limerick Rd., Newark, DE 19702
(302) 731-7788
humaneanimalpartners.org

Florida
Caring Fields Felines
6807 SW Wedelia Terrace, Palm City, FL 34990
772-463-7386
cffelines.org

Georgia
Good Mews Animal Foundation
278 Smyrna Kennworth Rd SE, Smyrna, GA 30082
(770) 434-7929
goodmews.org

Hawaii
Oʻahu SPCA
(Honolulu; exact address on website)
808-356-2200
oahuspca.org

Idaho
Simply Cats (Boise)
Boise, ID 83709 (exact address on website)
208-343-7177
simplycats.org

Illinois
A.R.F. – Animal Rescue Foundation
531 W Roosevelt Rd, Wheaton, IL 60189
(630) 200-3828
arf-il.org

Indiana
Fried's Cat Shelter (Michigan City)
Michigan City, IN (site of converted motel)
friedscatshelter.org

Iowa
SAINT Rescue & Adoption Center
1200 16th Ave SW, Cedar Rapids, IA 52404
319-551-7537
saintiowa.org

Kansas
Great Plains SPCA
5424 Antioch Drive, Merriam, KS 66202
(913) 831-7722
greatplainsspca.org

Kentucky
Animal Care Society
1600 Lundy's Lane, Louisville, KY 40216
(502) 366-3355
kyhumane.org

Louisiana
Cat Haven (Baton Rouge)
11130 N Harrells Ferry Rd, Baton Rouge, LA 70816
(225) 636-2680
cathaven.org

Cat Shelters

Maine
HART of Maine
Cumberland, ME (check site for curbside/drop-off location)
hartofme.org

Maryland
Small Miracles Cat & Dog Rescue
10236 Baltimore National Pike, Ellicott City, MD 21042
smallmiraclesrescue.org

Massachusetts
Gifford Cat Shelter
30 Undine Rd, Brighton, MA 02135
617-787-8872
giffordcatshelter.org

Michigan
Ferndale Cat Shelter
23100 Woodward Ave, Ferndale, MI 48220
248-545-7683
ferndalecatshelter.org

Minnesota
Feline Rescue, Inc.
3500 Bloomington Ave S, Minneapolis, MN 55407
(see website)
felinerescue.org

Mississippi
Community Animal Rescue & Adoption (CARA)
Jackson, MS 39209
(see website)
bestfriends.org/partners/community-animal-rescue-adoption-cara

Missouri
Humane Society of Southwest Missouri
3161 W Norton Rd, Springfield, MO 65803
417-833-2526
swh.org

Montana
AniMeals No-Kill Adoption Center
1700 Rankin St, Missoula, MT 59808
(406) 721-4710
animeals.com

Nebraska
Hearts United for Animals
1000 Plum St, Auburn, NE
(402) 274-3679
hua.org

Nevada
Nevada SPCA
5375 S Procyon St #108, Las Vegas, NV 89118
(702) 873-7722
nevadaspca.org

New Hampshire
Animal Rescue League of NH
545 Route 101, Bedford, NH 03110
(603) 472-3647
rescueleague.org

New Jersey
Tabby's Place
1100 US-202, Ringoes, NJ 08551
(see website)
tabbysplace.org

New Mexico
Best Friends Animal Society NM
4421 Lead Ave NE, Albuquerque, NM 87108
(505) 855-9969
bestfriends.org/our-work/places/best-friends-albuquerque

New York
Tompkins County SPCA
1640 Hanshaw Road, Ithaca, NY 14850
(607) 257-1822
tompkincountyspca.org

North Carolina
Goathouse Refuge
5111 Old U.S. Hwy 64 W, Pittsboro, NC 27312
(919) 542-2177
goathouserefuge.org

North Dakota
Red River Humane Society ND
W 602 16th St N, Fargo, ND 58102
(701) 232-4454
rrhs.org

Ohio
Village Pets Rescue (Dayton)
1835 W Dorothy Ln, Dayton, OH 45409
(937) 425-7625
villagepetsrescuedayton.org

Cat Shelters

Oklahoma
Oklahoma Humane Society
7500 N Western Ave, Oklahoma City, OK 73116
(405) 286-1229 ext.1
okhumane.org

Oregon
House of Dreams (Portland)
Portland, OR 97294 (exact address on website)
503-262-0763
kittydreams.org

Pennsylvania
Humane Animal Rescue of Pittsburgh
6620 Hamilton Ave, Pittsburgh, PA 15206
(see website)
humaneanimalrescue.org

Rhode Island
Providence Animal Rescue League (PARL)
34 Elbow St, Providence, RI 02903
(401) 421-1399
parl.org

South Carolina
Charleston Animal Society
2455 Remount Rd, North Charleston, SC 29406
(843) 554-4141
charlestonanimalsociety.org

South Dakota
Second Chance Animal Shelter
24189 SD-34, Hartford, SD 57033
(605) 528-1400
secondchanceanimalshelter.com

Tennessee
Memphis Animal Services
5440 Shelby Oaks Dr, Memphis, TN 38134
(901) 379-3123
memphistn.gov/animal-services

Texas
Operation Kindness
3201 Earhart Dr, Carrollton, TX 75006
(972) 418-7297
operationkindness.org

Utah
Best Friends Animal Sanctuary (Kanab)
5001 Angel Canyon Rd, Kanab, UT 84741
(435) 644-2001
bestfriends.org

Vermont
Kingdom Animal Shelter
1161 Portland St, St. Johnsbury, VT 05819
(802) 473-3377
kingdomanimalshelter.com

Virginia
King Street Cats (Alexandria)
Alexandria, VA (visit website for street address)
(see website)
kingstreetcats.org

Washington
Seattle Area Feline Rescue (SAFe Rescue)
(North Shoreline, WA) (see website for exact)
seattleareafelinerescue.org

West Virginia
Animal Friends of North Central WV
252 Brewer Rd, Morgantown, WV 26508
304-290-4738
animalfriendswv.org

Wisconsin
Happy Endings No-Kill Cat Shelter (Milwaukee)
5349 W Forest Home Ave, Milwaukee, WI 53220
(414) 744-3287
happyendings.us

Wyoming
Kindness Ranch Animal Sanctuary
854 State Highway 270, Hartville, WY 82215
(see website)
kindnessranch.org

www.ingramcontent.com/pod-product-compliance
Lightning Source LLC
Chambersburg PA
CBRC090058100526
44582CB00013B/179